C000067100

The F... ...

This
Bible Story Time book
belongs to

_____

_____

_____

Text by Sophie Piper
Illustrations copyright © 2006 Estelle Corke
This edition copyright © 2014 Lion Hudson

Published by Lion Children's Books
an imprint of
Lion Hudson plc
Wilkinson House, Jordan Hill Road,
Oxford OX2 8DR, England
www.lionhudson.com/lionchildrens

ISBN 978 0 7459 6364 8
e-ISBN 978 0 7459 6817 9

First edition 2006
This edition 2014

A catalogue record for this book is available from the British Library

Printed and bound in China, July 2015, LH06

Bible Story Time

The First Christmas

Sophie Piper ✳ Estelle Corke

LION
CHILDREN'S

Long ago, in the little town of Nazareth, there lived a girl named Mary.

She grew up believing in God. She grew up wanting to do the things that are right and good.

As she grew up, she looked forward to getting married. It was all arranged that she would marry Joseph.

One day, an angel came to her with a message.

"God has blessed you," said the angel. "You are going to have a baby boy: Jesus. He will do wonderful things. People will say he is the Son of God."

Mary was puzzled. "I'm not married yet," she explained.

"God will make everything come true," said the angel.

"I will be happy to do what God wants," replied Mary.

Joseph was upset by Mary's news.

"Mary's baby isn't my baby," he said. "Perhaps I shouldn't marry her."

That night, he had a dream. An angel spoke to him:

"Please look after Mary and her baby. Everything will be all right."

Soon after, Joseph went to find Mary. "I still want us to be husband and wife," he said to her.

"Now, I know you've heard about the emperor – that he wants to have a new list of all the people in his empire.

"I want us to go to my home town of Bethlehem together. There we shall put our names on the list as a family."

When they got to Bethlehem, there was a problem.

"No one has any spare room," explained Joseph. "We have to shelter in an animal shed."

That night, Mary's baby, Jesus, was born. She wrapped him up snugly.

"This manger can be his cradle," said Joseph.

On the hills nearby were some shepherds. They were looking after their sheep.

They were watching for danger. Who could tell what lurked in the shadows?

Suddenly, the sky was bright.
An angel appeared. "Don't be
afraid," said the angel. "I have
good news. A baby has been born
in Bethlehem. He will bring God's
blessings to all the world. Go and find
him. He's sleeping in a manger."
Then more and more angels
appeared, all singing to God.

All of a sudden, the angels
disappeared. Everything was
dark again.

"Let's go to Bethlehem," said
the shepherds.

They went and found Mary
and Joseph and the baby.

Everything was just as the
angel had said.

Not very far away was the city of Jerusalem. Some people had gone on a long journey to see the king there.

"We're following a star," they said. "It is shining because a new king has been born. Is he here?"

The king frowned and shook his head. "There's an old story that the greatest king ever will be born in Bethlehem," he said.

"I want you to go there. If you find a new king, be sure to tell me where he is."

The men set out for Bethlehem.

"I hope this is the right way," said one.

"Oh look!" said a second. "There's our star again!"

"I'm glad we've come," said a third. "I think we've been very wise."

The star shone
down on a little
house in Bethlehem.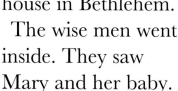
  The wise men went
inside. They saw
Mary and her baby.
  "This is the king we have been
looking for!" they said.
  They gave him gifts: gold,
frankincense, and myrrh.
  That night, they dreamed the same
dream. An angel told them not to
go back to the king. They agreed to
go home a different way.

Soon after, Joseph came hurrying to Mary and Jesus.

"I love you both so much," he said. "Now a dream has got me worried. I'm afraid we won't be safe here in Bethlehem. Let's leave at once."

The three of them journeyed on.

Mary held Jesus tight. After all that had happened, she felt sure of one thing:

Her little baby must truly be God's own Son, and she would keep him safe.